TBI – Our Never Ending Journey

AUTHOR: David & Sharon Marks

DEDICATED TO

My wife, two children and family support who were there before, during and afterwards to pick up the pieces and live with the after effects. Words cannot describe the debt that cannot be repaid in a lifetime; I will love you all for that always.

CONTENTS

ACKNOWLEDGMENTS

Without my wife looking into the order, missing parts that I had forgotten and filling the gaps I don't remember as I was in a coma and writing down the effect on the family we would have never even got this book finished.

PREFACE

This book is not about our trial and tribulations but more about the situations and the people involved in them. They all happened and only the names of the people involved have changed.

Because I don't remember too well there are things which I have missed out of the first book and because of that book people have reminded me of things which I should add in a follow up. Plus its somewhat informative to see what TBI recovery is like after two years and what is easier now and what it's like for my family and me.

1 THE ACCIDENT

When my accident happened, East Midland ambulance services were first on the scene. They arrived by helicopter and shortly afterwards were joined by road ambulance. I was a real mess but the people who helped me took it all in their stride with a kind of calmness. They had to make a critical decision very quickly. Use the helicopter to take me to hospital, which takes about three minutes or the road ambulance which takes about twenty minutes; the decision of road was chosen. Good job really as I suffered cardiac arrest twice on the way to Nottingham emergency room and there was not enough room to work on me in the helicopter.

I was in hospital in a coma for just short of a month and then moved from Nottingham to Derby where I spent another month in the respiratory ward and then a further four months in the rehabilitation ward, which is a total of six months in hospital before continuing my rehabilitation as an outpatient.

For some reason I thought that when I left hospital everything would be the way it was before and all the issues that i had would be fixed, only because there is only one way up from death and so you tend to progress quite quickly in the first six to twelve months and then the progress becomes a little slower.

The five main problems I have are:

1) Balance and walking
2) Talking
3) Sensory loss and pins and needles all the time on my left side plus my right hand
4) Double vision and weakness on my right side
5) Hearing impairment in my left ear

All of these things were caused by the accident and none of them have returned to normal.

2 NOTTINGHAM HOSPITAL

On arrival to the emergency room I was treated and then moved to the high dependency unit where the rest of my friends and family met me for the first time. I was in a coma so was pretty much non responsive and it was hard for them to see me as I don't remember much from the end of August 2011 to Christmas 2011 even though my accident was 30th October. The brain has a way of blocking things out which you don't need to remember, so it's probably best that I don't recall.

Because I was in a coma I was full of tubes to help me breath and pump pain medicine into me. It was hard for Sharon and my children to see me that way especially as the outlook portrayed by the medical staff was not very positive. At one point my wife had been asked if last rights where needed what member of the clergy had to be contacted. As you can imagine this did not go down well.

The medical staff in the National Health Service did a wonderful job; after all I wouldn't be here without them. They have to build a realistic picture of the incident; any better news is a bonus!

After nearly a month I was taken off the ventilator as I was able to breathe on my own so was moved into critical intensive care. I was still being fed by a tube, a sort of slim fast concoction. I could not speak due to the feeding tube so Sharon printed out an ABC chart and gave me a wooden spoon as a pointer. This also served as a grabber as I had two broken collar bones so my shoulders and arm movement was limited, it was invaluable to me and life would have been much more difficult without it. I used it on several occasions to press the buzzer as it was out of reach.

In one way I am really lucky, I am diagnosed with TBI, (Traumatic Brain Injury) but my family and friends stuck by me and a lot has changed for everyone. Also most of my permanent injuries are due to severed nerves and not physical or psychological. To look at me (if I was quiet) you wouldn't know there was anything wrong. The term `hidden disease` is very true, it's only when I speak or move about you notice that something is wrong. A funny voice and poor balance give the game away but some head injured people have complete personality changes and are totally different to their friends and family after the accident. I can comprehend what the therapists are saying and follow simple instructions; some injured patients are in a very different situation. There is excellent support for the patient with physiotherapy, psychology, speech and language and occupational therapy onsite at the outpatient head injury team.

3 THE DERBY HOSPITAL WARD (402)

I was still in Nottingham and this was nearly an hour away from home so for logistical reasons I was moved to Derby hospital into the respiratory ward. I remember the transfer as it happened very early in the morning and the bed in the ambulance was very hard, sort of like lying on a big piece of wood! This is the last vivid memory I have back to August 2011.

I had a catheter inserted into my bladder and the nurses used a Hoist to get me in and out of bed because I had some paralysis and couldn't yet walk. On top of this I was somewhat incontinent and had to wear pads. This situation for me was very degrading, I had basically gone from globetrotting executive to a fully dependant disabled person in less than 24 hours. It was like I went to sleep and woke up a different person. Every so often my breathing tube would clog up with condensation and the result was a banging noise from the pipe reverberating. This happened during the night shift at 3am. Before when this happened I was in a coma so it was really the first time I had heard it. I was still pumped full of morphine and now could hear a sound that was a lot like the drums from the film Jumangi, Because I was asking the nurses whether they could hear drums and they couldn't I thought I was hearing things. The tube was connected to my throat, six inches from my ear so to me it was really loud ! This noise combined with the morphine medication plus communicating via the ABC chart caused some confusion and eventually one nurse, trying to help picked up the tube saying "do you mean this tube?" The water ran down the tube and spilt all over my chest in a big puddle. I could have drowned, but at least there were no more drums.

My lips were really dry, I had sores all over them because of the tubes and the nurses gave me lollipop sticks with sponges on the end dipped in water, pineapple or orange juice to wet my lips. I was so thirsty that I use to suck on them. As soon as the sponge exited my mouth I wanted more. The children were very good and used to give me the lollipops.

A friend of mine had seen these sponge lollipops so he bought me a Calypso lolly. It was a great idea and tasted awesome but with hindsight was really stupid and dangerous, I was still learning to eat and drink so if some of the water had got into my lungs it could have caused an infection and put my rehabilitation back several steps. Anyhow I decided not to eat any more Calypso and pretended to choke; I was rolling around on the bed and pointing to my throat. He went white and was panic stricken, he just froze as if this was his worst nightmare. I carried on just long enough until he was about to notify someone and then just sat up and smiled. He was very annoyed, more with himself that he fell for it!

I was really drugged up. In total I was on thirteen different types of medication one of which was Morphine. As I mentioned before I thought I was hearing things and late one evening I was really hot so I had the fan on and the window open. Above this noise I could hear an owl, I looked at my wife and asked whether she could hear it too. "Yes, I hear it" and looked out the window. "Thank goodness for that, I thought I was going mad." The next day a friend of mine was sitting at the end of my bed on a chair. I saw him crawl up the wall and across the ceiling. I thought I had imagined it and when I looked back at where the chair was it happened again. It was on a Monday and the doctors were doing their rounds at 4pm. I asked them to go through my medications one by one and I didn't need it I got rid of it. I went from 13 to 3. Then the doctor came back into my room and said I shouldn't cut this particular medicine out as I would be in pain. So I went from 13 to 4 in one day, the logic was I'd rather have the discomfort than the hallucinations and hearing strange things. I was that confused I didn't know what was a dream and what was real life.

At one time I had fourteen student doctors around my bed asking different questions. You could see them all trying to figure out what was wrong with me. The head doctor said that you could see my muscle wastage in my legs because I had been in hospital for so long. I replied "I've always had rubbish legs it's nothing new!"

Once I had spasms in my all of my muscles. I was curled up in the foetal position shaking uncontrollably and all of my tubes came out. One of the Health Care Assistant stayed with me for two hours and told me to put my knees up and this would give me some relief. Just putting pressure through my heels had eased the muscles twitching so violently! Such a simple and easy thing to do that had made a big difference to me.

Whilst in hospital I contracted MRSA and consequently I was in isolation until I was cleared. As a precaution I was given a special air mattress which helps to prevent bed sores. This was very good but the motor made a whirring noise as it blew air in and out of the mattress which echoed around the room. I need total silence and complete darkness to sleep, so a combination of beeping from the feeding tubes, the mattress, the ticking clock, being drugged up on morphine next to a big window and not being able to communicate was a recipe for constant interrupted sleep.

A good friend of my father in law sent me a large get well card with a picture of Jesus on the front. It contained a Catholic blessing and at that time half of Ireland had a candle lit for me! I looked like Jesus on the card as I hadn't shaved for three weeks and because of all the tubes I had my arms always in an open embrace, all I needed was a halo and I had a complete costume as I was already wearing a hospital robe. The next day I awoke and when I saw the card I thought I was in heaven!

My daughter gave me a small puppet on a stand which moved when you pressed it underneath but I didn't yet have the strength to do it, so I left it on my table and this became my first goal! Seemed like a good one at the time so my sister in law bought me hand strengtheners for Christmas which I couldn't do either. I told this to my physiotherapist and she gave me three rubber ones each with a different resistance. I used it for the first time and used extra pressure as I had already failed twice so pressed extra hard. The strengtheners immediately snapped and like an elastic band flew across my bay into D's jug and knocked over a vase of flowers which consequently smashed and spilt water everywhere. I pressed the nurse call button.

During this time I had to relearn to eat and drink. Bearing in mind I had not eaten for two months I was classed as greedy. Everything tasted so good, it was blended but the flavour was incredible. Liquids were thickened with a powder, especially water and tea which was revolting so I flavoured it with orange or blackcurrant squash. As I got better I was accelerated to smooth and then fork mashed food.

When you take a drink or eat something you automatically swallow twice, this is called the second swallow. One day I went to Costa coffee with my family. The coffee shop was down stairs and I went in my electric chair. I had a mint hot chocolate and the girls had cups of tea. My wife ordered her coffee and four bacon rolls. I was used to eating and drinking on my own where I had only had to concentrate on one thing at a time. In the coffee shop there was lots of sensory information such as TV's, people talking, the children wanting attention etc. My brain could not close my gullet quick enough because it could only do one thing at a time and didn't do the second swallow. The result was that the hot chocolate had only one way to go and it came through my nose! It went everywhere!

As a test to move to regular food I had to eat a wheat biscuit without any water. It took me three tries but eventually I did it and dreamed that night of a juicy steak. The next day at lunch time I was given metal knife and fork and I stabbed myself in the nose with the fork. I calmly put the fork down and asked for a plastic one instead.

I had been in hospital for about two months and was complaining bitterly that I hadn't washed my hair. A young nurse who was very kind called washed my hair with a special shower cap that heated up and had shampoo in it. It was wonderful and for a few days made a real difference.

A combination of limited movement, poor coordination and lack of sleep led to frustration on a whole new level. I was watching Band of Brothers on a DVD player I got for Christmas and was trying to put disc nine into the machine. I tried for about an hour and finally took my wooden spoon and whacked the table. I cleared the table in one swipe and everything went on the floor, I was so angry, all my frustration came out all at once. The jug of water, the bottle of black currant, DVD player, DVD's etc. Etc took the force of my anger, I was covered in water, the bed was wet, and the contents of my table were all over the floor. Just then a nurse came into my room and asked "What are you doing ?", I replied "nothing", and she just picked everything up and cleaned me up and then asked what I was trying to do. So I told her and she put disc nine into the player, it took her about five seconds.

I had been hospital for close to two months and I had been washed by a method of bed bath which really means a flannel wash. I moaned about it for weeks and said it was inhuman, the reason I wasn't allowed to have a shower was because I still had MRSA and very poor balance and the chairs they had were not appropriate. One day a junior physiotherapist' borrowed a suitable chair from the stroke ward and gave me a shower, I will always be grateful for their thoughtfulness and kindness.

The shower was amazing, firstly because I felt clean but what surprised me was I found out about the sensory loss which was caused by my accident. On my left side I just felt the pressure of the water but no temperature; on the right side I felt the heat of the water. It was very strange to feel nothing on one side of your body and the heat of the water on the other side.

I was really out of it on morphine, it was so bad I was hearing things and hallucinating. In the end I couldn't take it any more as I didn't know whether I was coming or going so I decided to cut the medication, this was not to the liking of the doctor who said "You can't cut the pain medication you will be uncomfortable", he was correct and had prescribed it in my best interest. However I would rather have the pain than the morphine haze, so I cut my medication further.

After a couple of days I had an appointment at the splint workshop for my right arm to stop me getting what's called lobster claw. I was feeling a little sorry for myself when I saw another guy opposite to me. He was also getting splints done but on both his leg as he had lost them. I felt like a right plum when I only had one dodgy arm and hand. The ladies in the splint workshop are masters at what they do, I was watching the way they made the splints and it was incredible how and what they do.

I had been in hospital for two months now and had never seen the wall behind me. I know it sound trivial but I was really bored, I was so bored I counted the lines on the air conditioning tiles on the ceiling, 5,250. I had to go for an x-ray and the porter wheeled me back to my bay. It was another yellow wall with the buzzer attached and a sign that said "High falls risk". I was hoping for something really cool, not sure what, just something different and was really disappointed!

4 DERBY HOSPITAL REHABILITATION (KINGS LODGE)

A week later I was eating chocolate mousse and because I had poor coordination I couldn't get to the bottom of the carton. Therefore I put the carton in my mouth and tipped my head upwards to let the moose slide into my mouth, this worked really well. Sharon came into my room about two hours later and asked "Why have you got a brown smudge on your nose?"

I was woken up at 8am on a Sunday morning for breakfast. This was my new routine; I had two slices of toast, a bowl of Weetabix and a cup of tea. After about two minutes I looked at my cup of tea and there was only half a cup. I called over to the lady that served breakfast and said "Are we on rations now?" pointing to my half a cup of tea. She took one look at it and said "I wouldn't give you half a cup of tea, you have drunk it!" it was said with such conviction and insult I felt like a right idiot!

I was eating for about two months and for some reason I started to chew on the right side of my mouth. Then I said to Sharon "Oh they do serve hot food". I couldn't feel temperature on the left side so I thought they served the food was served cold.

One week later I was moved to Kings Lodge which is a specialist rehabilitation ward for brain and stroke patients. When I moved I was coming out of the medicine phase and ended up throwing up on myself and my bedding and the occupational therapy nurse who was with me fainted. I pressed the panic button with my spoon and seconds later two nurses came rushing in to my aide, I pointed down to the floor and said it's not me its her !! Later that day she explained that she was on rotation and only had a few weeks left on Kings Lodge. I asked where her next stint was and she replied "it's in surgery". I advised that if that didn't work out a career change might be in order.

I was having problems with my vision and the optometrist confirmed that I had a certain medical condition caused by the weakness on my right side. I asked what it was commonly known as and she said "Crossed eyed". I told Sharon that and she said "you don't look cross eyed!"

The next week the doctors and consultant came into my physiotherapy session and informed me I had a wonky head. "Is that a medical term?" I asked. I had to tell Sharon what was changed this week. Long story short your chin is supposed to be in line with your dip at the bottom of your throat which in turn lines up with your belly button. Mine doesn't because when I hit the lamp post I bent my spine into an S shape and I am consequently one inch shorter!

I never worked out whether it was my moaning and the medical staff wanted to shut me up or the fact that I was sick on my bedding but I was given a new mattress - one that didn't have either air or a whirring pump, I was very grateful.

When I first moved to Kings Lodge I had a shower and had to sit in a special chair to keep me upright. The first or second time I had a shower I sat in the chair and I had to over stretch for the shower gel and the chair tipped over and I hit my head on the tiled wall and bounced off the floor with the chair on top of me! The nurses came rushing to my aid and helped me get up and checked me over. I think my pride was more damaged than my head, but I had two big scrapes on my forehead, I sort of looked like Hell boy the next day. I didn't want to tell Sharon over the phone so when she came in the next afternoon she was obviously quite concerned. She asked "Where did you hit your head?" As I had two huge bumps on my head I thought it was quite obvious "My head!" to which she replied "I know your head, but where did you hit it! She obviously meant where I was when I hit it.

Soon after it was Christmas 2011 and was a really difficult time for me. I tried to make it fun for my family but to be honest I still had so much medication in my system it came and went as if it was another day.

A few days later I had my first physiotherapy session where several tests were conducted including a sensory test. I stood for the first time and it was then I found I couldn't feel my left heel when it landed on the floor however it was fairly strong. I could feel the right leg but it was very weak. At this point I was scheduled for a nerve conduction test. This is a ridiculous situation for someone trying to walk, if you really wanted to mess with someone this is exactly what you would do. I felt as if someone was trying to push me over the edge!

In Kings Lodge I was able to have a shower every day. The nurses were able to shave me every other day and eventually they asked me to give it a try myself. I remember thinking, shaving my face with poor co-ordination in my right hand and not being able to feel much on the left hand side of my face was not a good idea. However I gave it a shot and too my surprise I was pretty successful at it. Later that day Sharon came in to see me and after about thirty minutes later asked who had shaved me today. I exclaimed proudly "I did". Sharon never said a word but a little bit later I passed a window and saw my own reflection; I had cuts all over my face and I looked like I had been in a fight with a knife.

In January I was finally cleared of MRSA and was therefore moved from isolation into a bay with two other gentlemen who were twice my age. This was one of the best things that happened to me as isolation was mentally very difficult.

I looked around me and was astonished at how small my portion of the bay was. My photos had been neatly placed on the wall pillar and my post it notes with Sun to Sat were on the wall next to my bed, this was important to me as it was the only way I knew who was visiting. Everything was laid out on my table and put into my wardrobe and then I noticed the large window on the other side of my bed, the clock above my bed, the other three mattresses were air and had whirring pumps, at the end of my bed was the sink where nurses washed their hands and the communal bathroom was next to me. I started to look for the candid cameras as I honestly thought now I was in some sort of social experiment and someone was messing with me. If I couldn't get to sleep in a room I had to myself I certainly had no chance in a bay.

The next week I had to go for an x-ray because the nurses thought that the feeding tube was not in place. I knew something was wrong because before the tube fitted in my pyjama pocket and now it was down by my waist. You don't have to be a rocket scientist to tell it was coming out!

One of the gentlemen was eighty two and the other was eighty three. At that time my voice was still very bad because of the tube which was in my throat so they both thought I was Polish. I let them think it I just simply didn't have the energy to deal with it at that time. A few days later I confessed that I was actually English and as originally from Warwickshire. They looked somewhat surprised!

It was on a Sunday morning and on the one and only time I slept and dreamt I was half awake and was planning what I would do on that day, shave, shower, drive to work etc. etc. Then I opened up my eyes and saw the yellow walls and thought to myself "shit ... I'm still here!" I was gutted just for a moment I had forgotten about what had happened.

At 3pm and 8pm every day a lady came round with tea, Hot chocolate, Ovaltine or Horlicks and a choice of either biscuits or slices of cake. At that time I didn't know what gave me an upset belly so I started switching out the caffeine for hot chocolate. I had never heard of 50/50 at that time so had never tried it. Half water and half milk with a spoonful of hot chocolate powder. Perhaps I was spoilt but I was used to 100% full fat milk and no rations on the chocolate. Let's just say I moved onto Ovaltine the next evening which was quite frankly disgusting so the next night I tried Horlicks which was as bad if not worse than the Ovaltine. Therefore I was back to the tea, after all if that was wrong there would be public outcry! Anyway I was off the tea for four days and I still had the crappers. At least this way I wouldn't be putting on much weight! Or so I thought. Each Saturday morning was weighed in day; I put on five pounds even though I hadn't technically eaten anything for close to a week.

The nurses do most things but they don't cut hair and nails. There is a company who does this and comes in except the waiting list is about three weeks. Ben had been waiting for six weeks and I'm not that patient. I waited two weeks for Sharon and then gave her a call and asked where the shaver was. I used a shaving mirror to see and plugged in the shaver. Adrian said to Ben "He's never going to cut his own air is he?" Just then I turned the shaver on and ran it straight across the top of my head. I figured that if it went wrong it would grow back anyway. I couldn't reach the back so one of the nurses helped me finish off. I cleaned up and turned to both men and asked 'Who's next?". You should have seen their faces!!

It was pancake Tuesday and my wife and youngest daughter brought in pancakes and sugar and lemon for me and the people in my bay. The nurses have a policy of not being allowed to reheat food for patients but family members can use the kitchen and do it themselves. This small treat was something traditional and different from hospital food which brought a smile to a few people's faces. It was well worth the effort, as Michael Angelou said "people may not remember what you said or did but they will always remember how you made them feel." I was very proud of my family that day.

In the morning I had about fourteen doctors around my bed asking questions and working out different hypothesis, you could see their brains working overtime! In the afternoon the neurology consultant came to see me and she asked "Are you OK?" Now bear in mind I had just come out of critical intensive care, a coma and was in an electric wheelchair you can imagine my response! She was just being cordial and asked the question at the wrong moment in time!!

The next day a man moved into our bay called Damian. Everything was okay until about 10pm, then he started to snore. This experience was a new level of snoring. It was even detectable from the nurses' station which was about 150 metres away. At 6am Damian got up and had a shower which was right next to my bed and made a horrendous noise with his fan making a whirring sound and then his bed squeaking when it moved up and down plus the bathroom door slamming and the noise of the shower running. This went on for the next three months. In order to cope with this I invested in neoprene ear plugs, construction ear defenders and an eye mask. I said to the nurses "Wake me up when we land!".

One evening Damian fell asleep and started snoring. Alan started to laugh and said it was even more difficult to sleep now. So I gave him a pair of ear defenders. Thirty minutes later Adrian and I were both wearing the defenders and a couple of weeks later I returned from physiotherapy Damian were gone. I asked where he had gone and found out that he wanted a window so he moved opposite a guy called Ben. "Not Ben with the tattoos?" I asked and the response was a "Yes". The next day Sharon came during visiting hours and saw Ben in his own room, "What are you doing in here?" she asked. "They moved Damian into my bay and I didn't sleep a wink, I said to the sister the next day "You either move me or him". So the next day they moved Ben into his own room.

I went to the day room where there was a selection of reading books. I found one which sparked an interest, with double vision I couldn't read for very long, but I tried anyway. So there I was reading "A near death experience" and watching Causality on TV, for those of you not familiar with Casualty it's an emergency room drama. A nurse came in and looked at the book and then looked at the TV and exclaimed in "You are joking right? With all you have been through do you really want your visitors to see that"? I suppose she had a point!

A few weeks later my consultant sent me for Nerve Conduction Testing. The doctor asked me to sit on the bed with my arms outstretched. He pricked my hands and arms with large needles; I said that I didn't feel anything. I had about six needles in my arms and the doctor said stop looking at the needles which I did and started to look at the single loops placed on each of my hands. One said "positive" and one said "Negative". "You're not going to electro", bbbuuuuzzz "cute me are you ?" I yelled out

. "I thought you said you didn't feel pain", the doctor said. "Yes but I haven't electrocuted myself in the last few months!!" I answered. The doctor spent the next two hours electrocuting me and when he finished I asked "So, what did you learn?" He answered "Your right arm is not as good as your left arm". I just looked at him and said "I could have told you that two hours ago and without the electrocution!!" Of course it wasn't that simple, there was a big report on which nerves were active and how active etc. I didn't realise it at the time but this report was a critical document in my therapy.

Sharon bought the new Apple iPhone 4s and it came all shiny and new and she migrated everything from her old phone across to the new one. To test it was working she called me. My voice was not easy to understand over the phone but with some practice and a finely tuned ear she could make it out. However I couldn't hear her, it sounded dull. I asked her to ensure the volume was turned up, we took the phone cover off, and she went to a different room in the house to see if she could get a better signal and called me back just in case we had a bad line - no improvement. Then I asked Sharon to count to ten, swapped ears and asked her to count to ten again. It was as clear as a bell the second time round. It was that my left ear wasn't working properly! All this time I thought it was her phone it never occurred to me that it could have been my ear! About three weeks later it was confirmed by the audiology department that I had hearing loss in my left ear. I guess it's obvious really, if you hit your head the outcome may be that one of your ears is will be affected, because of the weakness in my right arm I had to hold the phone with my left hand but use my left ear, this was somewhat cumbersome. I said to Sharon "Seems a bit of a coincidence that it's my left ear which has damage and the car passenger seat is on the left!"

The next day I was watching Mrs Browns Boys on the DVD player I got for Christmas and was laughing out loud when Adrian asked me what I was watching. I told him and said it was a bit blue and not everyone's cup of tea but he was welcome to borrow the DVD and player. The next day I asked him whether he could walk and come and get it "No" he replied. "Can you walk Ben", I asked "no" he said. "Well we're screwed then", I laughed. "Your twelve feet away and I can't get it to you! Press the nurse call buzzer".

Because I didn't speak for close to three months when I did start speaking it was with an accent and was close to inaudible. Consequently I met the head of speech and language who advised I was going to start therapy the following week. The head of department was from Iran and he spoke broken English. I was in my electric chair and I didn't say anything but was thinking you can hardly speak English and you're supposed to teach me?

I had a speech and language session with a student. The student was very good and I had to say short phrases ensuring I spoke with great clarity. My goal was to say the word "Slur" without slurring. The student that was working with me had a speech impediment herself and really struggled to say the phrases!

Because I had a brain Injury my speech had a slur and I had difficulty pronouncing vowels because the brain doesn't tell the tongue to move quickly enough. To remediate this I worked with a lady who helped me concentrate on practicing the right way to say letters, words and sentences. She was very good and had a speech impediment herself. So I was going to end speaking with an Iranian accent and with a slur! I was given homework and was seen about three times per week. I had to say words like "sneezes" out loud. As I was now in a bay the other patients thought I had Tourettes syndrome as I kept shouting out random words!

Seriously though if you imagine all the people in the UK with different accents, language and even sounds that do not exist in the English language this team needs to know them all and possess the skills / techniques to help people, it's an incredibly difficult job in which you need the patience of a saint as it takes a long time. I still speak funny and I recently met a lady from north Yorkshire who spoke with a Czech accent and she has never been to the Czech Republic!

One of the former patients bought the entire ward flat panel televisions. Therefore we all had our own TV's; this was very good as in between therapy sessions there wasn't much to do. What the person did was to buy twenty of the same TV's with the same remote controls. One evening I saw Ben watching Adrian's TV as well as his own. I knew there was some logic to it as he kept switching from his own TV to Adrian's and back again. Eventually I had to ask so I shouted over to Ben "What are you doing?", he replied "I'm watching two Football matches at the same time, whichever wins, gets the league cup", makes perfect sense when you think about it.

Each TV remote control operated the other persons TV and I had the master remote to tune the TV's in. This was not commonly known and the infrared signals bounced off the walls and ceiling. The result was people were forever switching the channel on other people's TV's, turning them off and adjusting the volume. Consequently the TV's needed re-tuning and so people kept borrowing my remote control. One afternoon I came back and my remote was gone, it didn't matter as I wasn't watching TV anyway but after dinner I started my usual routine, I knew I would want to turn the channel in about an hour so I asked one of the nurses to look for it. She spent about forty five minutes scouring the nurses' station and each bedside table. I eventually found it about two feet from me on my own bedside table, she wasn't amused.

Adrian was a charming fellow. He could just about talk anybody into anything. One day I looked over to his bay and he had one nurse on either side of his bed filing his nails. I couldn't believe my eyes. All he needed was someone fanning him with a palm leaf and he would have looked like Julius Caesar.

It was about 8:30pm and Adrian leaned over and picked up a birds cream cake box, removed a sausage roll and started eating it. I exclaimed "Hang on a minute, you can't just do that. Who do you think you are? Paul Daniels?" What he had done was asked his son to get it. On Friday his son brought him fish and chips from the local chip shop.

When I needed the toilet I was placed in a queue. This was okay for me as I had the bladder muscles to hold it in, if you are older your muscles are weaker and then it is more difficult. I was also in a showering queue and the first time I was in for 45 minutes for shave, toilet and shower. Everyone complained about the amount of time I spent in the bathroom. I thought it was quite good for someone who has poor coordination, can't feel his face and was in a wheelchair. What I didn't realise was that Adrian had taken a suppository at 8am which took 30 minutes to work. As you can imagine I was not popular. The next day I did everything in 29 minutes!

The queuing system did not work for the elderly and was too late for Ben and it was too late for me when I had the Delhi belly but in both cases the incident was handled with sensitivity and left the patient with their dignity left intact. It was a good job really as we all had the Neuro virus so we had constant sickness and diarrhoea. It was so bad that the medical people sealed our bay off with an inflatable door called the Derby door.

Because I was having sleeping difficulties I started taking a tablet to help which gave me the Delhi belly. Therefore I stopped taking the tablet and still had sleep problems so I asked the sister whether I could start sleeping in the gym. At first it was a no but then i mentioned that the hospital is supposed to be a place of rest and I am trying really hard with the eye mask, ear defenders, neoprene ear buds and sleeping tablets and no-one uses the gym at night-time!! She finally agreed. What I didn't realise that I had just added one more thing to the "To do list". When I went to the gym it wasn't until 10pm and then I went back to the bay at 7:30am. I got about five hours sleep in there because it was quiet.

Not long afterwards I was scheduled Occupational Therapy which basically reintegrates me into society and enables me to complete daily activities. In order to make use of my right arm I made tea and toast played dominoes. In addition to mechanical movement I was also assessed for cognitive deterioration but what would have made a real difference was writing. Because of the weakness and poor coordination fine motor skills such as holding a pen was very difficult. I am right handed so it would be my right which was affected!

Every night I instead of brushing my teeth I had to use mouth wash, this was given to me in a small plastic beaker. After a while I was able to administer my own medication and this included the mouthwash. I spent twenty minutes trying to get the top off the mouth wash bottle; it just kept turning round and round. That's when I noticed the child lock label!

I mentioned that I was not sleeping very well until I moved to the gym. I was fast asleep when I was awoken at 2:30am for a blood test. As you can imagine I was not at all amused and didn't see the bigger picture that this was a process of elimination. My reaction was "Who takes a blood test at two in the morning?" I was told the doctors name and my response was "Let's wake the doctor up and get him down here to take the blood."

Each night I was given an injection in the stomach to stop deep vein thrombosis (blood clots). Each injection gave me a bruise and it could only be given in the stomach. After I was in the hospital for about three months I had about 100 injections in the same area I said to the nurse "I now have more bruises than when I hit a lamppost at 70mph!" As the injections were aimed at the elderly and long term patients the next day I spoke with the doctor and stopped the injections as I was up and moving around now.

I went to the activity room and read the head injury leaflet on memory. I knew that something was wrong but didn't know what. I couldn't remember from the end of August until Christmas, it was kind of patchy up until the middle of January. It was all there I just couldn't access it, sort of like when you were born, you know it happened but you just can't remember it. I could remember some things with great clarity but others I didn't have a clue. There was a psychologist on the ward and he did an evaluation on me. It was very strange. I was in the top 75% for my stage of recovery and answered most of the questions pretty well. One of the tests was to follow a simple set of four directions within the room.

1) Go from the table to the door
2) Go from the door to the filing cabinet
3) Go from the filing cabinet to the window
4) Go from the window back to the table

I got to the door and couldn't remember where to go next. At the start of the test I was told to remember a color, the test was about 20 minutes long and when I was asked the color I couldn't recall it. However when I was asked whether the color was Blue, Black, Yellow, Green or Orange I knew straight away it was Blue. The result was that I was diagnosed with no impairment but had a touch of short term memory loss which the medical team were confident this would get better over time. The results would be used as a baseline and then six months later they would re-run the test and see if there was any improvement.

It was 2am and I was in a deep sleep when I was gently awoken and asked "Did you take your sleeping tablet Mark". I was very cross because I was having a lot of sleeping problems and my name was not Mark. I said "My name is David, if you can't get my name right how do you know my medication is correct?" The poor girl was only doing her job and replied "Sorry I have short term memory loss." This made me even madder and I responded "You know you have short term memory loss when you have to put the days of the week on the wall!" The nurse looked to the left and saw my post it notes which told me the days of the week and who was coming when. She apologized, asked her question again and then left.

Each table had a jug of water on it. With a combination of weakness and poor co-ordination I couldn't pick up the jug if it was full, only if it was about a quarter full. One morning I was very thirsty and was trying to be patient but it didn't work so I tried to pick up the jug and ended up pouring it all over myself as it was too heavy and my right arm shakes when I grip something tightly. I pressed the Nurse Call button and they helped me get changed, replaced the bed clothes, poured some water into a glass and mopped up the floor. The jug held about nine pints / 1.2 gallons of water and went everywhere! About three hours later Sharon did exactly the same thing. I just said "I have a brain injury. What's your excuse?". The glass of water didn't seem that important anymore.

Due to my poor coordination and weakness eating was particularly difficult and I still needed my food cut up and its been over a year over a year later. It was lunchtime and I was really hungry so ordered vegetable soup and sandwiches. It came on a tray and as I was in a bay my curtain was closed due to someone being hoisted to the bathroom. I pulled the tray towards me and picked up the spoon. I dipped it in the soup and my arm started to shake, I dropped the soup. So I tried again, this time it went on the bed, I don't give up easy so tried again and the soup went all over the floor. I was really hungry so it seemed to be a good idea to hold the bowl with two hands and tip it up to my mouth. The result was that the bowl started to shake and went all over me, the walls the curtains everywhere. I pressed the Nurse Call button.

On Valentine's Day there wasn't much I could do so I went to the shop downstairs and got a card and a box of chocolates in my chair. Sharon turned up with gifts for me, chocolate shaped hearts in a box and a card plus a silver heart engraved with "I love you". I had physiotherapy in the morning and Sharon was waiting in the day room. For the first time I walked with some help into the day room. It was very emotional for Sharon and I plus the physiotherapist.

Because I had sleeping problems sleeping I was scheduled for Relaxation and breathing class. This would kill two birds with one stone as I also kept running out of breath when speaking and sleeping. I was wheeled into the gym in my bed, there was about another six people already there and I was the last to arrive. The room was dark and there were fairy lights on the ceiling, whale music was playing in the background. We had to do certain breathing exercises and mark out of ten how relaxed we were going into the session and then afterwards, 10 was very stressed and 1 was very relaxed. I was asked at the end of the second class and had to be awoken to be asked.

There were medication rounds at breakfast, lunch, dinner and 10pm. The nurses were always late which wouldn't normally matter but because my sleep was all messed up and I was in pain. So when they came round at 12:30am I was asking how the process worked. Basically to not cause any confusion the nurses always go round the ward in same order and this helps not to mix up medications, they start with the women's bays first and then move onto the men's. At that time there were 16 men and 2 women, so one of the women's bays was empty. The people who were handing out the medication were the sister and the senior nurses. Therefore I took the opportunity to mention that it was taking a long time and ask where we were in the list. I found out we were last and suggested that our bay was moved to the women's ward, after all there weren't any women in there. The response I got was that the reason there were no women there is that they never get sick. At which point A said "the reason there is so many men is because they do all the work".

Each week I went to Costco coffee on the bottom floor in my electric chair. You would think that if the tables anywhere would fit electric chairs a hospital would be the place, however the Praline & cream coffee was so good that it no longer seemed important. What was interesting though was that I had spent so long in isolation that being in a busy coffee shop was a complete nightmare on many levels. It was like sensory overload, just too many sounds and people in one place for me and I just couldn't cope with all the stimulus.

At that point I had been in hospital for nearly four months and spent two of those trying to get a straight answer about when I would get better and how long I would be in hospital for. You see I came from a world which was highly measurable and A+B=C it was logical and straightforward and I was now in the medical world where A+B may equal C or D or E or F and its different for every patient so it's not at all a linear equation. So when my neurological consultant didn't answer my questions I snapped "Okay give me the MRI scans and X-rays and I will do it myself". Four weeks later I got the scans and had a walk through from one of the doctors. I had no idea what they meant; it just looked like a bunch of blurred dots to me, rather like a baby foetus picture. At one point I was holding the picture upside down, I really had no idea. The people who do this work really truly are experts in their field! if you are reading this and have or know someone who has a TBI take solace in the fact that you're in good hands, even if it doesn't make sense just take their word at face value and do what they say.

If you're in the neurological field and dealt with me this is a formal apology for being arrogant or rude at anytime during my stay at Derby Royal hospital during October 2011 to April 2012.

I had to relearn to walk and Physiotherapists were teaching me. I used to walk by stepping. One physiotherapist told me to put one foot in front of the other rather than stepping. This is a small but obvious piece of information but when you have a head injury you have to start from the beginning.

In order to walk properly you need good core stomach muscles, balance and coordination. That makes sense, but in order to speak you also need good breathing technique. It sounds silly but physiotherapist and speech had to re-teach me to breath. I had to be told that when you breathe in it makes your belly go out. This sounds odd to me because when the phrase "suck your belly in" is used you breathe in. I was running out of breath because my diaphragm was weak. The team gave me exercises to help me and it worked!

You have to be organized to have a head injury as everything takes longer. One of the things which had happened was that I no longer had a switch that tells me when I'm full I was gorging myself. I once went over to The Mallard pub and ordered a mixed grill (for two) and ate the whole thing!

There were two signs above my bed; one said "High falls risk" and the other said "Nil by mouth". I was located right in the middle of ward 402. Opposite the food cart, therefore I could smell the food; I could see the food but couldn't have any. This was like a form of Chinese torture, I was so hungry and the slim-fast concoction was just not cutting it, to give you an idea at how bad this was I lost 25% of my body weight, my dog now weighed more than me!!

At Kings Lodge I was assigned an electric wheelchair. I was assessed as being able to navigate the hospital and use the chair, so that evening the chair was taken away and charged. It was brought back the next morning and after I had my breakfast and got washed and dressed I was transferred to my chair. Part of my stomach exercises was to sit in my chair for two hours in the morning and two in the afternoon. I pressed the button to go forward and the chair shot across the room and took the plaster and paint off the wall. I reversed and the chair shot backwards and hit the other wall. I assumed that reverse would be slower than forward. What I didn't know was that when the chair was charged it was put on warp factor nine and was left there. The next day I had Bumpers installed in my room. I said to the maintenance man "Not only can I not handle a 200 mph motorbike I can't handle an 8 mph wheelchair either!"

I had the electric chair for about three weeks and it had a mechanism on it which allowed you to disengage the wheel and use it as an attended wheelchair in case the batteries failed. One day I was coming back from visiting hours when one of the nurses stopped to talk to me. When I wasn't looking she engaged the fail safe on one of the wheels on my chair. When we finished talking I went to drive off but ended up going round and round in circles, I said this is nothing new I've been going in circles for the last decade!

On the weekend I went to the Mallard pub. After getting washed and dressed for the day I had to order my slot to get out of bed using a device called a rotunda. This is a machine which takes two nurses, one to hold the machine steady and one to help you stand up and rotate you 180 degrees so that you can easily transfer to a wheelchair. To get there my wife pushed me from the hospital to the pub. She had to go across a pedestrian crossing which had a slope down towards the road. We pressed the crossing button and were waiting for the flashing green man to appear which told us it was safe to cross when Sharon's mobile phone rang. She let go of the wheelchair to open her bag. In the meantime my chair started to roll down the slope. It was cold that day with a biting wind so I had my hat and gloves on plus my hood up, therefore I didn't hear the phone go off and I thought she was joking around as earlier on I had joked "Just push me into the road and get it all over and done with". It was not a small road or slow road to cross but Sharon realized just in time and grabbed my chair, a second later and it would have been messy!

If you think about it, when you hit your head really hard an ear or an eye if not both are bound to be damaged. Anyway I was waiting for my eye appointment at the hospital. Because I had double vision I couldn't use an electric chair and because I had broken both shoulders I couldn't use a self propelled therefore a porter kindly pushed me to the waiting area and checked me in. I was sitting in my chair waiting when I saw an elderly woman being pushed it a chair to waiting area. Then she hopped out of the chair and walked twenty feet with a cane across to the reception desk and checked in. I couldn't believe it, it was a miracle, and she was cured! Then she came and sat on the chair next to me, big mistake. I asked her what the stick was for and she answered "I can't walk very far", she said. "Where did you park?" I enquired. "Car Park 3", she replied. "Where are you going afterwards?" I asked "Home" she said. "Oh and you will park on the drive?" she answered "Yes". Less than 15 feet from her house and the car park is 50 feet away, I said to myself. "So that cane is just for sympathy then?" I said. Provocative, argumentative maybe but I was stuck in a wheelchair and I couldn't walk so this drove me really mad!

Sharon bought the new Apple iPhone 4s and it came all shiny and new and she migrated everything from her old phone across to the new one. To test it was working she called me. My voice is not easy to understand over the phone but with some practice and a finely tuned ear she could make it out. However I couldn't hear her, it sounded dull. I asked her to ensure the volume was turned up, we took the phone cover off, and she went to a different room in the house to see if she could get a better signal and called me back just in case we had a bad line - no improvement. Then I asked Sharon to count to ten, swapped ears and asked her to count to ten again. It as clear as a bell the second time round. It was that my left ear wasn't working properly! All this time I thought it was her phone it never occurred to me that it could have been my ear! About three weeks later it was confirmed by the audiology department that I had hearing loss in my left ear. Its sort obvious really, hit your head one of your ears is bound to go. Because of the weakness in my right arm I had to hold the phone with my left hand but use my right ear, this was somewhat cumbersome. I said to Sharon "Seems a bit of a coincidence that it's my left ear which has damage and the car passenger seat is on the left!"

Just after learning to eat I had my first meal "chicken a mornay". I couldn't wait, when you have been fed by a tube for the last three months directly into your stomach everything tastes good. I picked up the Knife and fork eagerly and promptly stabbed myself in the nose with the fork. I put the metal cutlery down, pressed the buzzer and asked for plastic ones instead.

I was in physiotherapy and the senior lady asked me to get on the floor and try to crawl like a baby. Easy I thought and so I tried it. It took me a while just to get on the floor and then in the right position for crawling. At this stage of my recovery it is normal to be fatigued after exercising but I was absolutely wasted. I thought it would be easy but it was the most physically draining thing I have ever done in my life.

Because my spine was bent into an S shape I had three vertebrae which were rotated 90 degrees. Therefore my physiotherapy session involved three additional people holding me a certain way whilst the physiotherapist pushed the spinal bones back into place with her thumbs. Because your neck is so close to your ear the popping sound seemed really loud. Are you okay she asked so I checked to make sure my fingers and toes still moved and replied "Yes I'm fine, carry on". Now if I screw up in work no one is going to get seriously hurt. If the medical people mess up some might be permanently paralyzed. That's when I realized the difference between important and critical. A tough way to gain perspective but a valuable lesson.

I was asked to attend a two week training course called the Bobath course. This had two benefits, firstly I would get two extra sessions of physiotherapy per week and secondly I would get more people to understand my condition and perhaps identify different approaches. The course was about a 20 min walk from the ward and using three elevators, two buildings and three different floors. I was a little apprehensive about this journey so to prepare I did a dummy run the morning before and had the hospital ward number set into my phone as an emergency. I was so preoccupied by getting there on the first day that I couldn't find my way back! I spent nearly an hour going round in circles trying to get back to the ward!

The Bobath course lasted two weeks. I did the first day of the second week but then had to pull out because I contracted sickness and diarrhea. I suppose it would be pretty embarrassing if thirty five people all came to Derby hospital and went home with sickness and diarrhea!

After a while in rehabilitation I started to part take in Occupational Therapy which combines a set of skills and strategies to prepare you for the outside world. The first thing we did was make a cup of tea & toast. This sounds a little funny but you need to be able to know how high to fill the kettle, which arm to use to lift and pour the milk, the order in which things are done and how to butter the toast. Sounds easy but when you add weakness, poor coordination and confusion into the mix things become pretty tricky! I still can't carry a cup of hot tea from one room to another, its just not safe, I will burn myself. Next up was playing a game of dominoes. The movement of shuffling and setting up the pieces would help better understand the range of movement my hands, arms and shoulders had, on top of this was a cognitive assessment which would give the therapists a baseline to work to and measure whether things were improving and at what rate. After I had made several cups of tea, beaten all of the therapists at dominoes and completed the cognition test I asked "when will you teach me to write?" This is important to me for birthday and Christmas cards, the doctors, opticians, recording recorded delivery and filling out all the government forms. The therapists tried lots of things but to avail. Because of the weakness to my right side, plus the poor co-ordination and the nerve damage to this date my writing looks like 4 year olds! In the end Sharon downloaded writing exercise from the Internet and I am teaching myself by playing Pictionary and drawing with the kids.

In Kings Lodge at night time you were given mouthwash instead of brushing your teeth. For some reason I was no longer given mouthwash so I bought my own in the chemist downstairs and also brushed my teeth. The first time I did this I spent nearly 20 minutes trying to get the top off the mouthwash before I realized that I had been fooled by the child lock!

5 GOING HOME

Soon it was time to leave the hospital and go home. This is done in stages one of which is to put the patient on level one which basically means ensuring that the person can self subscribe their own medication. This for me was quite a good thing because it meant I didn't have to wait for the nurses to come round I could do it myself. I had medicine at 8am, 1pm, 6pm and 10pm. The medicine was kept in a locked cabinet next to my bed and although I had the key I couldn't get to it because it was out of reach, so I relied on someone to unlock it and pass me the medication. Then I would take it as I usually put the whole day separated into small plastic beakers at 8am. One evening the nurses didn't come round for the 10pm medication until 12:15am so all the people in my bay were waiting except me as I was able to self subscribe. I asked why they were so late and the reason was that one of the other patients had an issue which took a long time to resolve and that this bay was the last on the list. The medicine cart went round the ward in a clockwise rotation so I suggested that they go anti-clockwise. However so that there are no mistakes the same route is always used. "So where does the route start then?" I asked. "In the women's bay" came the reply. "If there are only two women patients and two bays why don't you just move this bay then?" The answer was not what I wanted to hear so I just gave up.

The weekend before you go home you have a trial run to see if you can get in the car and identify any issues with going home before you are discharged. I did a trial run on a Friday and going back to the hospital on the Sunday evening. It was a great weekend for both me and the family. When I got back to the hospital on the Sunday I was weighed and that's when I found out I had put on ten pounds! The food at home was much more flavorful than at the hospital.

When you have a head injury your perception of speed and distant is all over the place therefore the government deem you unsafe and revoke your driving license.

I hadn't been in a car for six months when my wife came to pick me up from hospital. I thought she was driving really fast as the world was rushing towards me. I kept yelling "watch out" and pressing the imaginary brake pedal. On top of that because I have weak stomach muscles my head kept snapping back and forward as my wife accelerated and braked, I kept saying she was kangaroo jumping but it was just me. It's a good job my driving licence was taken as there is no way I could drive!

When I got home Sharon made a special meal. The table was set with the glass of water on my right. Normally this wouldn't be a problem but I was so glad to be home I forgot that my right shook when I gripped something in my right hand. After eating for about ten minutes I reached out for the water. My hand started shaking so violently that water went everywhere. All over me, the table and everyone at the table. I looked at Niamh and she had water dripping off her eyebrows. I drank what was left in my glass and asked whether I could have a dry shirt.

Being at home was great except for one thing, biting my tongue when eating. I pretty much bite my tongue three to four times per week. Because I had sensory loss I couldn't feel my left cheek and lips so I didn't know the location of the food in my mouth so when I chewed I consequently chewed my tongue.

I had been in hospital for around six months and had been accustomed to eating on my own with poor co-ordination. In trying to get the food to my mouth I had picked up several bad manners along the way, such as drinking from soup bowl. When I moved to a bay with other people I was speaking with mouthful, eating too quick in order to get to my next therapy session on time etc. Etc. The long and short of it was that I ate like a pig. So the first time I set down to eat dinner my dinner my family looked at me in complete disgust.

One rainy day we had a paper plane making competition. Once they were made we had some practice flights and then the competition, the winner was the person's plane which went the furthest. The youngest daughter went first and the eldest daughter both went a respectable 20 feet. I went last and was confident I could at least match their efforts after all my plane was aeronautically designed and had excellent dynamics plus balance unfortunately the person throwing the plane (me) didn't have either. I moved my left arm back and got the angle just right and then thrust it forward with such vigor it could easily fly the 20 feet it needed to win. I did however forget one small but important point, to let go of the plane. I lost my balance, threw my legs behind me as if I was on ice skates and face planted on the floor crushing the paper plane as I went. I lost that competition!

Because I was in a wheelchair I couldn't do too much as it was an attended chair and needed to be pushed. However what I could do was online auction buying and selling. All the stuff that was in the house and garage which was no longer being used was sold on auction. I made about three hundred pounds selling things which were just sitting gathering dust. I would go into the children rooms point to something and ask "Are you using that, because if not I'll sell it!" I also bought things, mostly things I could do with the kids. I purchased Chess sets, Xbox games, Giant snakes and Ladders etc. One day I got sick of tripping over shoes lying around so I bought a shoe rack. It came about two days later, but two came instead of one. I checked the quantity and I definitely only ordered one. It took me all afternoon to build it and I broke the first one so used the second one as spare parts. It lasted two days and fell apart. Sharon super glued it back together and lasted another two weeks and then collapsed. Its without a doubt the worst thing i have ever bought !

I start to get some feeling back in my nerves. This like a very strong feeling of someone walking over your grave. The doctor said this was a good sign and was my muscles going into spasms. One evening my hand jumped off my leg and hit myself in the head. "What did you do that for?" Sharon asked. "I'm glad you asked that, I thought I imagined it!" I replied.

When I first went home I was sleeping downstairs. I converted my dining room into a hospital bay and I thought at last I would get some sleep and enjoy my family plus get some routine back in our lives. The first few nights was settling in so I didn't expect to get much sleep. But a after a week and thing had started to quieten down I could hear this whooshing noise in the makeshift bedroom. At first we thought it was the water pipes in our house and then we realized it was the noise from next doors central heating boiler starting up.

I have private medical insurance and so arranged an extra physiotherapy session at home. The first session I used the gym ball that Sharon had at home. I sat on it and my phisio said it wasn't filled with enough air. So we pumped it up and tried again. The phisyotherapy said "I was too heavy for that gym ball". I was 155lb's before my accident, 110lb's after two months of eating through a tube and lying in bed and 185lbs when I got out of hospital. "are you saying I'm chubby ?" I asked my phisio.

It's amazing how quickly your body is willing to adjust or compensate for a change. When I got home I still couldn't walk, didn't have good balance and couldn't go up the stairs safely. The hospital is a very safe l place, by and large it's all on one level and if you need to go to another level there are elevators, electric doors etc. When you're at home you have to negotiate different surfaces such as carpet, tiles, steps, Patio doors, uneven surfaces such as grass, paving slabs and different gradients. One afternoon after therapy Sharon was wheeling me back to the downstairs dining room which we had temporarily converted. We got to the door way and I just got up and strolled across the room. "Where are you going?" Sharon asked. "I don't know" I said and promptly fell onto my bed. I had forgotten I couldn't walk!

I had been at home for around six months now sleeping in our makeshift hospital room which our old dining room every time I went in or out of the front door / dining room / kitchen or the living room they were staring at me. It was a Friday afternoon and I had physiotherapy at 2pm at home. Lisa arrived and asked what I wanted to do "core or legs / balance today?" to which i replied "i want to try going up them" pointing at the stairs. I reckon with your determination you could get up, I don't think you could get down safely." hmm "Good point i hadn't thought about coming back down. Perhaps I'll just stay up there then. Everything is already there - bathroom, TV etc. I'll just get Sharon to bring up my meals and medication!" Lisa looked at me and quietly said "Not many people fall up the stairs, most accidents are on the way down!" I thought about this for a second and came to the conclusion that it could be unsafe, however the world is full of if's, buts' and maybe's so I decided with some confidence that I was going to take the risk so I said to the physiotherapist "I'm going to do it but I would prefer to do it with you", and at that I went up the stair for the first time in over a year. Seems silly really but it was like a whole new world was opened up!

It was coming up to Christmas and Sharon's birthday is in December plus my two daughters are in January and March. Therefore cards needed to be written and posted. This sounds like a straight forward task but if you cannot write it's somewhat difficult. Therefore I used an on-line application from my phone as I just tapped the screen which was easier than pressing down keys on a keyboard. It's a little impersonal but it worked. This way I could also send a gift as well, sounded like a good idea. A cousin of Sharon's used to call me religiously every two weeks and did so for close to six months so I sent him and his family a Christmas card and a box of Truffles as a small token of my gratitude. I didn't realise that the truffles box had a heart on it and was meant for romantic occasions. As you can imagine her cousin thought I was coming onto him. Thankfully Sharon sorted that confusion out.

Things which I have done before seem straight forward but new things are very hard to learn. The first time I realised this was when my seven year old brought her homework to me asking for help. Before I would know almost intuitively where to start, the structure and critical path to follow to get us to the end. The homework project was about habitats in your back garden. My daughter and I did pretty much nothing for two days until the day before the deadline and then Sharon came upstairs and did it in about ten minutes. It was difficult it was just new!

Being at home made me talk more, 1:1, on the phone and in a small group at the bus stop for example where I used to pick up my daughter. This was good in one way as I had different accents and personalities to deal with. The conversations are easier in one way because they mainly involved talking about me which I'm pretty good at. In fact that's part of the problem because I haven't done anything else for twelve months but be in this situation. When on another subject I found it quite difficult because I kept forgetting words. It was like the words were on the tip of my tongue; I could describe what I wanted to say but couldn't get it out. My eldest daughter asked whether I was now getting a stutter now!

Because I had sensory loss on the left side of my body this included my butt. This combine with not being able to walk very fast meant I had to go to the bathroom straight away. We have a bathroom downstairs and upstairs. My eldest daughter got home from school at 4pm and always went to the downstairs bathroom. Normally this would not be an issue but on that day I had diarrhea and I left it to late and found the downstairs bathroom locked. I tried to get to the upstairs bathroom but could not move quickly enough. I thought I had wind but unfortunately that was the day that I found out that farts did not have lumps in!

I was in the bathroom finishing up and when I reached for the door lock the knob came off in my. There was a piece of metal poking out of the lock which the knob slotted onto. I pushed the knob on but it only fitted on one way so the tube just pushed back towards the door and the knob fell to the floor leaving me locked in the bathroom. I called to my daughter and after about 15 minutes she pushed the pin back though and I unlocked the door. It was a good job I was not in the house on my own !

Because I had sleep problems I had to keep a sleep diary which documented how much / little sleep i got. I instilled a routine at home which left me wiped out. It went like this:

Monday - Physiotherapy & dishwasher

Tuesday - Polishing & dishwasher

Wednesday - Bathroom cleaning & dishwasher

Thursday - Speech & dishwasher & hover downstairs

Friday - dishwasher & clean food bin

Saturday - Exercises & dishwasher

Sunday - Exercises & dishwasher

Everyday exercises x 2 except mon & fri

Every am - speech exercises
Walking Tue, Wed, Thursday, sat and sun for a short distance with Omnotrain.

I only had to vacuum the front room and I was wiped out.

When you have a head injury you think you do things you can no longer do. The first thing the hospital does when you have a confirmed head injury is take your driving license. The reason for this is because your perception of speed and distance is all over the place. It makes sense as if you're not safe yet then for everyone's sake it's the best thing to do. I want to go to the gym and as I can't drive I thought that I would go on a push bike. I suggested this to my physiotherapist who had some questions:

(1). Who will help me on the bike before I go to the gym?

(2). Who will help me get into the gym and help me get on and off the equipment?

(3). Who will help me on the bike after I have finished at the gym?

She then explained that riding a bike required better balance than walking. Also you have many things to think about such as position on the road, braking, other road users, traffic lights etc. Etc. Etc. sounds easy but after I listened it was obvious I hadn't thought this all the way through. On reflection if I was struggling to walk the length of the kitchen and could only do one thing at a time (eg. Walk not walk & use a smart phone) there was no way that I could use a bike! This is quite typical of someone with T.B.I, they don't always know their own limitations and so have to be told. I have spent the last 12 months being told I can't yet do stuff and why.

I had been home for around six months now sleeping in our makeshift hospital room which our old dining room every time I went in or out of the front door / dining room / kitchen or the living room they were staring at me. It was a Friday afternoon and I had physiotherapy at 2pm at home. L arrived and asked what I wanted to do "core or legs / balance today?" to which i replied "I want to try going up them" pointing at the stairs. I reckon with your determination you could get up, I don't think you could get down safely." hmm "Good point I hadn't thought about coming back down. Perhaps I'll just stay up there then. Everything is already there - bathroom, TV etc. I'll just get Sharon to bring up my meals and medication!" L looked at me and quietly said "Not many people fall up the stairs, most accidents are on the way down!" I thought about this for a second and came to the conclusion that it could be unsafe, however the world is full of if's, but's and maybe's so I decided with some confidence that I was going to take the risk so I said to the physiotherapist "I'm going to do it but I would prefer to do it with you", and at that I went up the stair for the first time in over a year. Seems silly really but it was like a whole new world was opened up!

There is stuff I can't do that Sharon now does. Simple things like carry a hot drink from one room to the other and take things up stairs. Some things are really obvious like playing football and sports such as badminton others are not so obvious like walking in the snow, on grass, walking whilst using a smart phone. I learned the hard way and ended up falling down every other day, then week, then month. One day I was walking to the toilet and had my phone in my hand. I was so used to walking and emailing I just didn't think it would be hard. Then I just lost my balance and whacked my ribs on the kitchen work surface, this silly mistake put me back two months in my therapy.

6 THE HEAD INJURY DEPARTMENT

The reason I was able to write this book with poor coordination and double vision is the release from Google of the nexus 10. I originally got the nexus 7 for Christmas. Yet after I used it I found the keyboard to small. Google graciously accepted the device back and I purchased the 10 version. The reason this worked for me was that although I couldn't write or type, tapping the screen was possible and I backed everything up to Google Drive so if there was a problem I had a copy of the document.

I was booking a holiday and it was pointed out that it was a bit pointless if I can't go in the sea or swimming pool, on the beach or just exploring the area will be more difficult with a wheelchair never mind navigating the airports and the beach etc.

I went to the physiotherapy session the following day I asked for a six month plan to not miss another summer. I said imagine you had no resource or financial / time constraints, what would you do? I put a timeline on it and said I wanted to be able to walk a half mile with good balance. That day I went to the gym and that weekend I found a local gym buddy.

It's quite interesting really. I have gone from one extreme to the other! Every month I would be away in another country. Now I go to hospital and back. Sharon has done more miles in her car in the last twelve months than in the previous decade!!

There was a group therapy session for speech and language called "Survivor Skills". There was about nine people in the room and it was a little like an alcohol anonymous meeting. Each new person had to introduce themselves and briefly talk about their accident. One patient introduced himself and detailed his accident whose wife ran over him and pushed him through two brick walls. I tried really hard not to smirk but couldn't control myself when he pointed to his permanent tattoo of a tyre mark across his side.

I started to do more physiotherapy at home in the form of floor exercises. At first this sounds pretty straight forward but with a brain injury you have to be told and shown the steps to be completed. I was on the floor doing exercises three times a day everyday for nearly three weeks. One day I forgot the process all together and got on the floor the way you would do if you didn't have strength, balance or walking issues. I fell onto my bottom with a thump!

Each Thursday I attended Speech and Language to try and correct my accent, slur and construction of sentences. At the same time I was try to read night time Dr Seuss stories to my daughter during the bed time routine. This was pretty ambitious considering they are rhyming, tongue twister books. At that time of the evening I was quite tired as well so my voice was extra poor but my daughter never said a word, even though she probably couldn't make out any of it!

It was coming up to my wife's birthday and Christmas and there was one thing I wasn't looking forward to as I was not very good at it and it took a lot of time. This was the writing and mailing of cards. I still couldn't write very well and all you need is an incorrect postal code and it won't get delivered. I therefore decided to put all the names and addresses into an on-line card website and do it from there. The card is the printed and mailed from there, a bit impersonal I guess but I didn't have much of a choice as I couldn't yet write. There are people who have never received a Christmas card from me and the family who are probably quite surprised!

When I first got home we were not sure what we were going to do for money as in three months our income would go to zero and we didn't get any benefits. I had a little time on my hands as we were given a settling in / adjustment period of six weeks. So we decided to join an on-line buying / selling auction and prioritized this spare time very simply into things which would bring money in and things which would send money out. We gathered the things together which we no longer used such as toys, clothes, electronics, bicycles, shoes & boots etc. Then we sold them on a on-line auction. I used to go into my daughters room and point to stuff and ask "Are you using that?" We did pretty well, brought some money in and gave some joy to kids as well!

7 THE SERIOUS STUFF

All joking apart this really is a big issue. I am really lucky, I have a head injury but my family and friends stuck by me and a lot has changed for everyone. Also most of my permanent injuries are due to severed nerves and not physical or psychological. To look at me (if I was quiet) you wouldn't know there was anything wrong. The term "hidden disease" is very true, its only when I speak or move about you notice that something is wrong. A funny voice and poor balance give the game away but some head injured people have complete personality changes and are totally different to their friends and family after the accident. I can comprehend what the therapists are saying and follow simple instructions, some injured patients are in a very different situation and while there is decent support for the patient with physiotherapy, speech and language and occupational therapy there is not enough in place to assist the immediate family. This wouldn't matter too much if it was a small number of people but there are over one million cases in the UK each year.

Not only is the frequency of occurrence increasing but patients are living longer which means they require longer term care which is tailored to each case. I don't have the answer but I do know we are talking years and months not weeks and months in rehabilitation and this costs. The reason this system is working is because of the dedication and commitment of the people who work in the NHS (National Health Service) in the UK, but this does not mean it is efficient. There are some very smart people in the medical community and I am sure that they will get the answer; I just hope it comes sooner rather than later.

Remember once you have a brain injury there is no "Fix", it will get better and life will improve, it will be different but not quite the same

8 THINGS I HAD FORGOTTEN

After my accident I had to go for lots of CT and MRI plus X-ray scans. The MRI scan involved having a box around my head and was very noisy. The whole thing took about 45 minutes and resulted in a whole host of images which I bought partly out of curiosity and arrogance but which turned out somewhat useful as they formed the front cover of this book.

I used to hold onto the bed rails and pull myself to the top of the bed because I kept wriggling down to the bottom. The Physiotherapist saw me do this and went mad. She told the nurses to remove the rails from my bed.

In order to put my trouser on in bed I would bridge. This involved me pressing my heels downwards while my knees were raised upwards and pointing towards the ceiling. This would create a space between the bed and my bottom and would allow the nurses to easily pull my trousers up. I thought this was quite helpful but when the Physiotherapist saw me bridging she went mad and said I was supposed to bridge. I asked "Why?" and was told that I didn't know how to. "So teach me", I replied. That was the end of that conversation.

I probably wasn't a good patient. I was always asking "Why?" which means everything longer because there is a lot of explanation. But if I didn't understand the logic or if it didn't make sense then I would want to know more. With hindsight things would have been much easier and quicker if I'd just kept my mouth shut!

When getting washed and dressed I had to use my left hand (which was stronger than my right) to put my deodorant on. When it came to under my right arm I would ask one of the nurses to do it. This was usually in the bathroom and because I had just showered the room was all steamed up. One of the nurses was helping me but because of all the moisture in the air her stick on eye lashes were coming off!

As I mentioned I had been to X-ray many times. But the most frequent occasions was because of the loss of my feeding tube which went up my nose and directly into my stomach. One morning I awoke to find it was nearly out altogether. I went down to in x-ray to photograph it and find out where it was. I knew it wasn't in far enough because the tube used to fit in my pyjama breast pocket and now it was down by my waist. On the first and second X-ray you couldn't see the tube because it was transparent so the team filled it up with a blue liquid so it would show up in the photo. This worked and the conclusion was that the tube wasn't in far enough!

Everyone does a second swallow automatically. If you have a brain injury your body has to relearn these responses, otherwise the following scenario happens. I was in Costa coffee drinking hot chocolate when I tried to do two things at the same time (drink and talk). I didn't do the second swallow and the hot chocolate liquid came out of my nose and all over my shirt. it's not a good look !

When I went to Costa coffee I was in my wheelchair but the chair did not fit underneath the table so consequently I knocked over all the coffees and hot chocolates we had just bought. You would have thought that if Costa would have tables that fitted wheelchairs anywhere it would be in a hospital. They do make good coffee though and their cake is wonderful.

I had the second swallow nailed so I went to Costa again, this time I got a take out coffee so I didn't have to deal with the table issue. I took a drink of the coffee and it came through my nose again. I did the second swallow but the take out cups have a hole in the top which you can suck the liquid through, my doctor told me that my brain is not quick enough to tell the mouth to move from the sucking position to raise the palate and close the airway in time, so consequently I don't use straws either.

Because I couldn't feel my left cheek and lips properly I was forever biting my tongue. At first this not bothering me but as time went on it got really annoying especially when I was really enjoying the food or was hungry.

When you have a brain injury you have to start again and learn everything from scratch. I mean everything from breathing, eating, walking, talking, moving your muscles and even selective muscles and that includes the muscle you use to control your bladder and to evacuate from. Therefore I had to wear a pad which is sort of a diaper/nappy and catheter insert for my urine waste which went into a bag hung to the side of my bed. I didn't have much street credentials before my accident, now I had none ! I really hated the potty training part and could not wait until it was over. It took me about three weeks, every time I was changed I would ask. Unfortunately at the same time there was a bug going around the hospital which caused sickness, from both ends. When you can't feel sensation on the left hand side and you have muscle weakness on the right things are very difficult. Needless to say there were a few un-savory clean up jobs!

Because I couldn't walk yet to get me in and out of bed and to go to the bathroom the nurses used what is called a hoist. This a sort of lift which is wrapped around your thighs and attaches to a sort of crane device which stands beside the bed. Then the nurse presses a button and the machine lifts you up. There is no other way of doing it but when you need the bathroom your trousers and pants have to come down first so you can go straight onto the toilet. What this means is that your butt and family jewels are hanging down for the world to see. The nurses try to make it better by closing everyone else's curtains and putting a gate across the bay but it is still quite degrading. But there is no other way of doing it.

I still can't click my fingers. It requires strength in the little finger and co-ordination.

When I first came home my wife adjusted the car seat for me as I didn't have the balance to lean over without falling over into the foot well. As I was unable to move car seat forward I would sit in the front passenger seat. My wife had her car for two years and she loved it. It had leather interior and was the sport model so everything was colour coordinated. To get in and out of the car I would sit on the seat and swing my legs round by ninety degrees. After about two weeks Sharon saw the scuff marks on the leather from the studs on my denim jeans pockets. The next time I got in the car there was a special rotating cushion too help me get in and out !

Because most of my meal times was alone and due to my poor co-ordination I developed bad manners as I was more concerned with getting the food into my mouth than how it was done. When I got home I was eating with my family and therefore had conversation to deal with, rather than just concentrating on the one task. I had a nasty habit of speaking with mouth full and because I couldn't get all of the soup I would drink from bowl. This is when you're on your own but when you're trying to teach a 7 and 12 year old manners it doesn't look very good if the daddy is eating like a pig.

You have to be organized when you have TBI. I have forgotten my medication so many times I now keep spare medication in the glove box of the car. I am so used to packing a suitcase that I used to be able to pack in ten minutes flat. I went to pack the other day and I had to empty the case four times to see if I had enough clothes and I was only going for three days ! It`s really amazing, things take so much longer now and it`s always the simple things which catch you out!

I played pool for the first time in two years. I thought it would be fairly straight forward. Boy was I wrong ! Firstly you have to make your way round the table, then remember which color balls you are and then hit one ball off another using a long stick. Sounds straight forward right? Well throw poor coordination, double vision, bad balance and limited range of the right arm into the mix and it's a complete nightmare. I played three games and lost all of them and that's with the other person giving me a chance. Perhaps I'll putt buying one on hold until I recover more !

During the pool match I needed the bathroom. I gingerly made my way across and opened the door. This was no mean feat as the floor went from wood to carpet and then to tile each separated by a threshold and bathroom door was attached to one of those things at the top which makes it close afterwards so getting through the door was more difficult. Once inside I noticed that each urinal was a the standing up variety. I hadn't stood up to go for two years so I thought I would try it. The result was nothing, I had forgotten when you have TBI you can only do one thing at a time so concentrating on standing and urinating and aiming at the same time is not going to work. In stead I sat down on the regular toilet and we had lift off !

I able to walk, just not very well and not for very far. In order for my heart and lungs to get some exercise part of my routine was going to the local gym. I was just going there to use the bike but found that there was as much social benefit as II was talking to people other than the medical community.

In order to make my recovery as successful as possible I started having physiotherapy at home once a week. I started out using Sharon's gym ball at the first session but I didn't realize there were different sizes and weights. I sat on the ball and squished it right down and landed on the floor, the therapist looked at me and said "I think we need a bigger gym ball! "

When I was an in-patient at Derby hospital I went to group therapy. It was weird at first everyone was in their wheelchairs and in a line in front of a target. We were given a small ball to throw at the target. This seemed really easy and then I tried it. I knew what to do but my body just wouldn't do as it was told. I aimed and threw the ball but my hands didn't let go and the ball just remained in my hands. I tried it maybe four or five times with the same result. It was so simple and yet I couldn't do it. I felt like when Spiderman kept getting things stuck to his hands because of the Spidey web !

After i was released, i mean chucked out, i mean discharged, i was an out patient at the head injury team in the old hospital. I attended a group speech and language therapy session which was a bit like an alcoholics anonymous session to be like. Each week a person arrived they stood up and said their name and what had happened to them and what they were looking to gain from the group. The new guy turned up and he introduced himself and then told everyone why he was here. The man had been reversed over by his wife and then pushed through two brick walls. I was keeping a straight poker face while he told us how long he was in a coma plus hospital etc. Then he lifted his shirt and said "Now I have a permanent tattoo" and displayed the tyre mark across his torso. At which point I collapsed with laughter, I couldn't contain it any longer and I just burst. I apologized profusely as you shouldn't laugh at someone else's misfortune but for me that was really funny.

As III learned to eat things became easier but I still had problems with peas, sweet corn and shredded wheat. These foods all got stuck to the dangle thing at the back at the back of my throat causing a gagging reflex. So many times people thought I was choking so I just gave up eating in public in case someone tried to do the choking maneuver on me, with 18 broken bones including all my ribs it`s really not a good idea!

After I was moved from Nottingham hospital to Derby I started to have physiotherapy and after the second or third session I started to muscle spasms in my legs. A spasm is the contracting or tightening of a muscle at a very rapid pace. This happened every three or four minutes for over an hour and a half. A young healthcare assistant stayed with me during this time whilst I was not "In control". She asked me to raise my knees up towards the ceiling and this helped. It also helped when I had spasm at home, they were less severe (17 incidents in about an hour) but in front of my family who are not use to seeing these things and were frightened as they didn't know what to expect.

Because I was being fed by a tube my weight went down to 8 stone 3lbs (or 11lbs in American money) I was so skinny that when I first stood up it was in front of a full length mirror all I could say was look at my knees ! They were massive !!!

I made my wife a cup of coffee, just the way she likes it. I carried the cup into the next room but by the time I got there the cup was half full. My balance was so poor it went everywhere and I used my left hand which was strong and well coordinated but didn't feel anything. The result was that I burnt my left hand. When my wife saw the cup she asked "Are we now on rations?"

In MotoGP Marco Simocelli a young Itallian motorcycle rider passed away in a tragic collision. There was an article in a national magazine which I had purchased for this article. It was written in the usual magazine style with three columns per page. I didn't know it at the time but reading in columns is almost impossible for me. I don't know whether it was double vision or my memory but by the time I got to the end of the second page I had forgotten the first page. It was very weird as I was used to never forgetting my keys, wallet or cell phone and now I couldn't read a short article on a great motorbike rider, I still can't read that article !

Because I used to travel quite frequently I was used to packing my suitcase in about ten minutes for weeks trip. I went on a three day trip to Ireland and packed case my case four times, each time I couldn't remember whether I had enough clothes. So I emptied the case and started again !☐

Because of my poor coordination my blackberry was very hard to use as the keys were to small so Sharon bought me a new larger more simple phone. I still couldn't write but could tap the keys on the phone so I could write down things as I still had problems remembering. I had a discharge meeting when I left hospital and there was a new persons at this meeting who didn't introduce himself and nobody knew who he was. I was messing with my phone trying to find my notes when he asked "was I going to record this meeting?", I replied "of course not." And one of the physiotherapists asked "Have you seen David's phone?".

Because of the swelling in my hand and me putting on about thirty pounds now my wedding Ring and dress watch don't fit me any more. Sharon says that my wedding finger is now rejecting my ring !

I was that tired that beneath my eye was a pulsing muscle due to fatigue, this was another added to the list!

When I first got home I got in the the car put the seatbelt on and it was uncomfortable on my broken collar bone and ribs so for nearly two year I wore the seatbelt across my lap and then instead of over my shoulder I put the belt under my arm. It was only in the last month that I wore my seatbelt normally.

For Christmas my sister in law bought me a new pair of slippers as my old pair broke when I caught my foot on the threshold. It doesn't sound like it would make much difference but walking in narrower slippers is much harder when the ones you use are much wider.

After my anger management issue with the DVD's I was asked to join relaxation therapy. This involved deep breathing and listening to whale music. I am not making this up we had low lighting and fairy lights ad everything. At the end of each session we were each asked to rate from 1 to 10 how relaxed we were before the session and afterwards. I was asked too rate my experience, after I was awoken so I said 8 on the way in and 1 at the end !

I was also invited to another group therapy session where I had to throw a ball at target and got points for now close I got to the centre. There was five of us lined up in a row and I was fourth. The two things I remember was that I was really rubbish and that I was playing against a Indian cricket fast bowler. The fast bowler won. When it was my turn I threw the ball and was surprised that even with poor coordination and weakness I managed to forget to let go off the ball!

It was winter and the kids were looking outside at the snow. I felt so bad because I knew they wanted to go outside and have fun in the snow. Snow is not easy to walk on as it moves under your feet and when it becomes compressed it turns to ice which id's slippy. I shouted upstairs to them and asked if after lunch they wasted too go outside and have a snowball fight. I was rubbish, my hand to eye coordination was awful, I think I only got two shoes on target but they seemed to have fun. I was soaked!

9 THERAPY – TWO STEPS FORWARD & ONE STEP BACK

The first achievement I had was when I was in Nottingham hospital and with the aid of two physiotherapists, my friend and my wife I stood up for the first time. Everyone was quite emotional as they were not sure what the outcome would be. I was so out of it on drugs I didn't know where I was or what I was doing!

Because I have sensory loss on my left side it is easy for me to burn or cut myself without knowing as I can't feel temperature or pain. This s particularly true for shaving as I can't use my right arm due to poor co-ordination (I am right handed) I have to use my left, however with some help and a little practice I managed it.

I hated using the commode to help me go to the toilet. The reason for it was the toilet seat was too low for me and the seat did not have handles so it was not as safe. I didn't care I didn't want to use it so I tried the toilet seat and it was worked out okay. The same applied to our three piece suite, it was too low. It was a bit of a struggle but I tried it and managed to sit okay. However I used to use the commode with the basin attached to wash myself as I couldn't yet get up stairs. This worked quite well so I continued to use it but it took me ages nearly an hour !

After about four months using the commode I finally got fed up as I never felt really clean. So I ordered a shower chair and with some help from Sharon I climbed into the shower and got cleaned up. This was a great feeling and made a world of difference, I felt human again. Not long afterwards as I gained strength and stamina the next step was standing in the shower so one day I just tried it and each time it got easier.

Once I could stand I was walking with a fame which made me stoop over so I quickly moved onto walking with a stick. The stick saved me lots of times, if I didn't have it I would have fallen for sure. What the stick didn't do was help me get good balance so walking on cobbles, grass or slopes etc and I couldn't walk very far.

I was released home with an attended wheelchair which Sharon had to push, it was heavy and at that time so was I. If you sit down or lie in bed for twelve months and people keep bringing you biscuits and chocolates your bound to put a little weight on, I put on about thirty six pounds. The wheelchair was made from steel and was heavy for my wife to get in and out of our car. Therefore when my physiotherapist said I could now use a self propelled wheelchair we jumped at the chance and bought a lightweight aluminum one. It seemed easy enough, just push the wheels and you go forward. Except when your left side is stronger than your right. Because of my head injury I had significant muscle wastage on my right side. The result was I went round and round in circles!

After nearly one year out of hospital I was able to Put on my boxer shorts while standing up. This may seem like a small step forward but up until that time I had to sit down to put my shorts on as I could not stand on one leg and I would get dizzy. I still needed to lean on something to steady my balance but I could do it.

When I first got home my coordination was so bad I couldn't Put the dogs collar on. It takes two hands to close the clasp and the weakness was so severe that I simply didn't have the strength to press the catch.

Only recently I gained the ability to thread my trouser belt. It seems so easy at first but it requires two hands and the ability to turn around 180 degrees around without falling over. When I first attempted this I didn't realize how difficult this was and went backwards hitting my arm and ribs on the side of the bed. I won't do that again in a hurry!

I wish I could cut my own food. Because of the weakness in my right arm I can't press down hard enough on the knife to cut tough food like meat, soft stuff is no problem but in a restaurant it is quite embarrassing when your forty years old and have to have your food cut up for you.

At first I couldn't tie my own shoes. What happened was that we needed to get back to school shoes for our girls so we went to a shoe shop and the girls were trying some on when the assistant said instead of looping the laces once or twice try three times and then the knot will stay put! I tried it and bingo it worked. One thing made easier!

I still can't cut my own nails on my left hand of feet but I can do my right hand as I have good strength and coordination with my left hand. Sharon does the rest for me which she hates doing and calls me a big baby as I complain when she catches my skin. She says I can survive a motorbike accident but getting my nails cut is a major deal !

When you hit your head hard sleeping becomes very difficult because the brain no longer produce serotonin which is the hormone which ceases brain activity and puts you to sleep. Therefore you take sleeping tablets to do the same job. I don't like sleeping tablets but thrust are a means to an end and better than no sleep at all. Unfortunately the pills I had been given conflicted with some of my pain medication and only worked until five in the morning and then I was awake again, therefore I came off them. The result was I didn't sleep so I tried coming off the pain medicine which was uncomfortable but I got a better night's sleep, the lesser of two evils I suppose.

We booked to go to Ireland for my uncles 40th wedding anniversary. I needed to rearrange my therapy as we due to be flying at 1pm so would be pushed for time. So I told my therapist and she asked whether I had got permission from my consultant. I had flown so much I never thought about it and just booked it. Apparently a bruise on your brain heals much slower than a bruise on your arm and when you go up in a aeroplane your ears pop at ten thousand feet because of the pressure in the cabin and this is not good for a bruised brain. Makes sense if you think about it just never occurred to me.

I was advised by my consultant that I couldn't drink alcohol for two years. I pointed to my wife and asked "have you meet my wife ? She is over there with the red hair, she is Irish, two years I've got no chance !". Alcohol kills brain cells so if you have a brain injury then drinking alcohol doesn't make sense.

When I first got home I didn't have the strength to pick my daughter up. After two years of hard work and guidance from my physiotherapist I can now pick up my daughter. I now have the balance when standing still to pick up daughter.

I am still much easier to understand face to face but over the telephone there is also an improvement. Speech and language have done a wonderful job especially when you compare my voice to twelve months ago. Even so the Tax man still did not understanding me on the phone and wouldn't talk to my wife on the phone as she did not have power of attorney. Even though I would be able to provide security clearance over the phone they couldn't understand me so they wouldn't do it. Now my voice still sounds funny but the tax people can understand me on the phone!

Because of my poor balance there wasn't a lot of fun things I could do with my children so i got a American Pancake & a Toasted sandwich maker for my birthday and Christmas. This way I could sit down in the kitchen and cook fun things with the kids.

I can't write but I guessed with some practice it could be done. I drastically underestimated this task both physically and mentally. In December I purchased a book for Valentine's day. The idea was I would write in the book every day until February 14th and then give it to Sharon. The book asked questions about your relationship like where you meet and things like that, I figured that if I completed one page a day I would be finished in time. Sounded like a good plan except I hadn't accounted for fatigue, birthdays, Christmas etc and 14 days before valentine's day I realized that I had some serious work to do to get it finished. I managed it but learnt a valuable lesson, you simply can't operate at the pace your used to and everything takes longer when your brain is firing on two out of eight cylinders!

When I first got home someone had to adjust my car seat. Now I can adjust the car seat myself, admittedly we have a different car now that is easier so I am not sure this is an achievement but I'm hailing it as one as I need all the wins I can get!

I was having vacuous sleeping problems. This is quite common with head injury survivors as the brain stops producing a hormone called serotonin which makes you go to sleep by reducing your heart rate and slowing your breathing. I was able to sleep with medication each night but didn't feel rested three next morning and looked as if I had big bags under my eyes.

When I look up the stairs I go very dizzy and have to sit down. Also when I take my tablets I take a drink of water but when I tip my head back I get dizzy to. One of our toilet seats was broken so I purchased a new one and set about putting the new toilet set on. To do this I had to kneel down and look up to unscrew the old one and screw the new one in. I felt so dizzy I was sick and I was just glad I was in the bathroom and didn't have to far too walk!

This has only happened to me once and has never happened to me again. I spoke up and felt really energetic just like before my accident. I did load that day and felt a great sense of achievement. I didn't have my usual crash at three o'clock and went all the way to ten o'clock and sleepy until eleven o'clock the next day. When I awoke I felt like I had just done a twenty four hour flight, absolutely knackered. Next time this happens I will better pace myself and perhaps the impact will not be so poor.

I could speak and be understood pretty well in a one on one session so I thought that communication in a group wouldn't be an issue. It never occurred to me that this would be some what difficult. There was nine people in the room and I just went to pieces. I was used to speaking in a tomb with ten time the volume of people bust it sounded as if everyone was talking at the same time and I didn't know when to speak and when I did people kept talking over me and not letting me finish. It was not at all a nice experience.

A person with Brain injury does things very slowly so if we went to the store on the way to the hospital or home it was easier and quicker for me to stay in the car while Sharon went inside. I didn't really mind as I would use this time to continue writing this book. Because I spent some time in the car and we were parked in the disabled bay I noticed that some of the other cars didn't always have the right permit or most commonly no permit at all. As time went on I got more irritated with this and eventually said something to the person who had parked next to me. His reply was "I agree with you but I only park here when I'm getting beer and cigarettes", I couldn't believe what I was hearing and he was serious as well!

A little while after I got home I started taking care of myself from a cleanliness perspective. In the morning I exfoliate, shaved, showed with precision, moisturized, deodorize and the final thing was applying aftershave. I had two types of aftershave, the poor on and the one with the spray. For some reason I decided to use the spray one, directly onto my face. I don't know why but it seemed like the right thing to do at the time. The inevitable happened and I ended up spraying myself in the eye!

I was independent in the bathroom and one evening before bed I was getting ready which as usual was slowly when I could hear this noise which sounded like someone opening a roller blind. I carried on doing my thing when I heard it again. I didn't think anything of it so I just finished off dying my hands when I heard it a fourth time. I thought it was Sharon so I opened the bathroom door and expected to see her standing there but she was downstairs. So I turned to shut the bathroom door and that's when I heard it again and realized the house was my slippers rubbing on the bathroom floor, I felt like such a imbecile!

10 THE EFFECT ON THE FAMILY

The effect is easy to underestimate. The relationship between the affected and their family can be changed forever and sometimes help is needed to work through this. Various issues can arise due to a head injury. Sometimes they can be quite dramatic and sometimes they can be quite subtle. Personality changes can be the worse as your family can feel like they don't know you any more. A psychologist can help tremendously and so can Headway, the charity which is specific for head injured victims and their families. I had some personality changes but most were minor, Sharon will tell you more about how the family felt:

To say the least it's been hard . When you see the scene played out in a movie , you never actually think it is going to happen to you . Police knock on the door , listening to what he has to say , the heart wrenching cries that are coming from your children , and your silently dying inside trying to keep it together for everyone, but its happened so now we have to deal with the outcome whatever it may be . Our lives have done a complete 360 , everything has been adapted , adjusted to the new life style we have . Changing from a wife to a caregiver, our children who have also changed from daughters to helpers, but through out have never grumbled for everyday we are thankful that we have David with us and all the changes are worth it.

David's personality has changed slightly, being meticulous about certain things and the fact that things need to be done at almost that very minute he thinks about it. We work around these things to please everyone involved and eventually get to meet both ends amicably. I'm having to play both roles now, doing David's jobs and mine and I'm tired more now than I have ever been but its best to keep going for if I have to much to time to sit around I think I will eventually break down and not be able to keep it up . The children miss there Daddy, he was the father you would see racing in the park with them, playing on the swings, kicking a ball and just 100% involved with their everyday activities and life. Now they have adjusted to daddy just watching and it's sad as I know it affects them and David. All we can do is continue the best we can, help David through his recovery and do things that will involve the girls and David doing more than just watching, and continue being a strong family unit, then the effects of David's accident will soon dwindle away and the life we are living now will be the normal way of living for us.

10 THE EFFECT ON THE PATIENT (ME)

One physiotherapy session I asked of all the people you have seen in the last ten years what is their balance like now? Silly question really as everyone is different and progress is very hard to measure. I got a generic answer with lots of soft words like "if and may" nothing concrete or hard. So I asked the question a different way. "Will I be able to pay badminton or squash again ?" "Probably not" came the reply. What about play football with the kids in the front garden? "Probably not" was the reply again. This was not what I wanted to hear and to make matters worse I was pretty sure that Sharon was of the opinion that eventually I would get 95% better and this summer would better than last and next year would be better than this year. I was pretty upset as I had not come terms with this at all and imagined that there was some sort of fix and that I wouldn't be in a wheelchair for the rest of my life. After a week I told Sharon and as to be expected she was also upset. This time however I was pissed off. We didn't deserve this and neither did our girls so I was even more determined now. Not to prove the medical community incorrect but to stop living this head injury journey and take back or lives.

I have got sensory degradation. This means that I have pins and needles down the left side of my body and I don't feel pain or temperature on this side either. This means the left hand side of my mouth doesn't taste much and because the taste is dulled spicy food tastes so good.

My broken shoulders had healed and my physiotherapist said I could now use a manual wheelchair, I didn't haves to be told twice, I went straight out and bought a lightweight one which was easy to put in the car and push. Because I had one strong arm and one weak arm I just kept going round in circles !

One evening I switched on the light and every light upstairs blew including to fuse. I could flick the breaker but was unable to change a light bulb as I'm not able to look up without getting dizzy, and the light bulb was up high and I couldn't stand on a chair because my balance wasn't good enough. This for me brought home the fact that my limitations were in fact limiting me. Sometimes it's the most simple things that can be the trigger and can bring home the situation to you. The same thing happened when we took the kids to the local park and I suddenly realized that I couldn't run around after them like the other dad's. I think that I had a touch of depression but Sharon was always able to turn a bad day into a good day.

Due to my right side weakness and crushed right shoulder I was walking like I had drank ten pints. In order to resolve this I had to do exercises three times a day. As these got easier more repetitions were added. At the point I was getting better at the exercises I suggested adding some resistance but was told that was not a good idea as it is better to do things well than to do too much and do some exercises incorrectly as you won't get any benefit.

I was getting about eight hours sleep a night and yet I still felt tired and had big dark circle under my eyes. I didn't know what was wrong so I went for a sleep study which involved me wearing a small monitor on my finger. The results were inconclusive and they scheduled a second sleep study where I had too wear an oxygen mask on my face. I just thought to myself why would you ask someone with a sleep disorder to wear something that is going to interfere with their sleep.

I was always a typical Virgo, a place for everything and everything in its place. After the accident I almost had OCD (Obsessive Compulsive Disorder). If I was following instructions they had to be exact, there was no messing around you followed them almost as if they were rules. Even if something was supposed to be fun it had to be right. If you were on the receiving end it felt like constant criticisms, but it wasn't meant that way it just came out like that. It was partly to do with the head injury but partly because my voice had constant tone, almost like a monotone robot, a cross one.

A robotic voice combined with a lack of patience made it appear as if I was angry and this was not the case and therefore I was continually explain my behavior. I was never patient but now I was really impatient. I couldn't help it, I had spent 39 years running at 100mph and now things took longer or I was with my kids who were doing things for the first time and they were doing their best it just wasn't my way.

I contracted MRSA and therefore was located in isolation for three months on my own. I stared at the yellow walls for such a long time I knew how many tile were on the ceiling and the number of gaps there were in the air conditioning grill. I thought about things a lot and was clock watching, waiting for breakfast or lunch, visiting hours or even medication round to break the day up or even someone to talk to. I think I had a touch of depression and was quite emotional. I had enough of the routine and just wanted to go home.

I was fed up with people telling me what to do. I felt like I was being treated like an idiot. Of course I wasn't but that's how it felt. I was kind of a control freak in a way. Usually I instinctively knew what to do and when to do it. In this world I had to rely on other people to tell me what to do and I was starting to get irritated with it. I remember I was going to take the dog for a walk just around the block in my electric chair and my daughter asked "Are you allowed to do that?". She only asked because she cared so I answered "yes, I'm Ok." But I remember thinking I'm 40 years old, I've been around the world, I reckon I can handle going around the block!

Because o my brain injury everything slows down and that includes moving your tongue from the back to the front of your mouth. This results in me speaking with an accent. I sound sort of Italian but I have had everything from South African to Australian and quite frankly I am sick of it now, I just want to be able to walk into a pub and speak without having people look and stare. It doesn't bother me but I know it makes the kids feel out of the ordinary.

I regret going out on my motorbike that day. I feel quite guilty about screwing things up so badly and yet the biggest regret is that I can't remember between the end August 2011 and the middle of January 2011. My accident was at the end of October, on a straight road and I was doing the speed limit. The camera was facing the other way and there were no witnesses so the only thing I can think of is a mechanical failure, oil or diesel on the road or some sort of debris on the road. I am not sure but it seems unlikely to be my fault.

If I was to have this experience again I would listen more. After all who am I to question the doctors. I don't know much about head injury and yet I had the arrogance to question their knowledge. I don't think so.

I was so hungry I ate fast and choked more, I would eat slower and put less food into my mouth. I would also refrain from speaking with something in my mouth.

I do a lot of talking and wasted a lot of therapy time. With hindsight I would listen more and talk less.

I am used to remembering almost everything. Not in a savant sort of way but in never forgot my wallet, keys, mobile phone or phone number etc. I used to remember all my parents car registration numbers right back to around age five and all our home phone numbers. Now I have short term memory loss so it's difficult to remember more than two things. This book for example was very difficult to write.

I was used to multi tasking for example walking and sending an email. I tried to walk and talk whilst going from the TV room to the kitchen and became really unsteady so I concentrated on one thing (walking) and things were better.

For my 40th birthday I had a few friends round to the house and we did a barbque. In total there were about fifteen people but I totally had sensory overload due to all the voices, music playing, kids running round and people asking questions. I think I did okay but for sure I was shattered by the end of the afternoon. The thing that really got to me is not being able to help out as much and not being able to go down to the bottom of the garden to eat as it is on a slope and my balance isn't good enough yet.

I am still not driving. Is been two years now and I still haven't been behind the wheel. This is a real pain in the but because if I want to go anywhere I am dependant on Sharon taking me there and she cannot be in two places at the same time. I think things would be much easier if I could drive.

ABOUT THE AUTHORS

David and Sharon have two children aged thirteen and eight and have lived in both the UK and USA but now reside back in the UK so they are close to friends and family. They are normal, everyday people who thought this would never happen to them but it has and the effect on their family has been devastating. Their whole life has been turned upside down however their outlook on life is to take the positive out of any situation, the glass is half full not half empty.

Many Thanks To:

The Nottingham air ambulance team and critical intensive care department plus the High Dependency Unit.

The Royal Derby hospital 401 respiratory ward, 301 Kings Lodge rehabilitation ward and the Head Injury Team (at London Road Royal Infirmary) therapists and medical staff who are not only helping me recover but taught me a life lesson about the difference between critical and important.

My friends and family that kept in touch came to visit regularly and called me religiously.

Tim for helping me speak so that my friends and family understand me.

Lucy for helping me with my physical and mental well being plus everything else that matters.

Mandy for help with our case and who went above and beyond the call of duty.

Anyone I forgot, there is GOING to be someone!!

Made in the USA
Charleston, SC
02 April 2013